Flash Boys, Wall Street and the Rise of the Machines:
Will Artificial Intelligence Cause Financial Meltdown?

By
I.K. Mullins

Brief, Concise and to the Point Publishing

Flash Boys, Wall Street and the Rise of the Machines: Will Artificial Intelligence Cause Financial Meltdown?

Copyright © 2014 I.K. Mullins. All rights reserved. No part of this book may be reproduced or retransmitted in any form or by any means without the written permission of the author.

www.ideas-facts-books.com

Table of Contents

Preface……………………………………………….5

1. Wall Street Goes Electronic and Algorithmic……..8

2. HFT and Its Algos Are Rising…………………...17

3. The Flash Crash and Other Surprises…………...21

4. Algos Go to War……………………….....……...27

5. Goodbye HFT, Hello HIT!……………………….34

6. Elementary, My Dear Watson!…………………..38

7. Artificial Intelligence Comes to Wall Street…......44

8. Google's Quest for Artificial Intelligence……….48

9. Artificial Intelligence and Financial Meltdown....50

10. Are We Forgetting Anything?.................................57

Glossary of Selected Terms...............................59

Preface

In February 2011, Watson defeated two highly experienced players in the game of *Jeopardy*. This victory drew a lot of attention in media because Watson is not a human being. It is a super-computer designed by IBM. And its arrival reminds us that the emergence of real artificial intelligence might be closer than we expected. For example, Ray Kurzweil, Google's director of engineering, thinks that, by 2029, machines could develop "consciousness" and the ability to do all the things that humans can do.

Will the rise of artificial intelligence affect our financial markets? If Watson 1.0 defeated humans in the game of *Jeopardy*, could Watson 2.0 defeat humans in the trading game played on Wall Street?

The current conditions of a computerized market and artificial intelligence research provide a glimpse into the market's future. And they paint a worrisome picture.

Since the rise of the machines on Wall Street, the markets have been behaving in unpredictable ways, going from one mini-crash to another. Neil Johnson, a professor of physics and an expert in complex systems and econophysics, calls these mini-crashes *"black swan extreme events."* They happen at time scale of a fraction of a second, remaining beyond human control. Johnson compares them to micro-fractures in a mechanical machine that can pave the road to its major breakdown.

Studies indicate that these black swans are caused by machine traders and computer algorithms fighting over the market. Today, regulators can neither monitor nor control them, and experts have difficulty understanding all the complexities of a market driven by computer algorithms.

If today's machine traders can have a negative impact on the market, then what can happen to the market in the not so distant future, when artificial intelligence takes over the trading floor?

In this book, written for the general public, we review the current developments that bring us closer to the first encounter between human investors and artificial intelligence traders. We take a look at some major players in this field and analyze opinions of various financial and high-tech experts. We also discuss the issues and threats to human investors that may arise from the computerized and "unmanned" financial markets, driven by this emerging artificial intelligence.

1. Wall Street Goes Electronic and Algorithmic

The ability to quickly process data and send it at high speed from one location to another has always been important for trading. Before the invention of calculators and computers, traders with the ability to do quick arithmetic calculations in their heads could easily outsmart their "less mathematically-gifted" competitors. As for speedy delivery of financially important information, messengers on horseback used to be the best bet. In the 19th century, carrier pigeons replaced them. And after that, the telegraph replaced the pigeons.

Information technology first arrived at the New York Stock Exchange in 1867 in the form of the ticker. Invented by Edward Calahan, it was used to deliver the latest stock prices to investors located away from Wall Street.

In 1878, the next technological advancement came to the NYSE in the form of a telephone. By the end of the 20th century, the old technology was replaced by computer-based trading (CBT). Computers began to perform tasks that were originally done by humans. They monitored a share price and issued trading orders in order to buy or sell the shares.

At that time, the computers did not make the decision to buy or to sell particular shares or another financial instruments. Humans were still making such decisions, and computers were simply executing the trades. Gradually, some trading firms began using more and more sophisticated computer algorithms (mathematical functions run by super-fast computers) to execute trades, and so algorithmic trading (AT) was born.

Computerization of the market has changed the speed at which trading is done and the time that investors hold a company's stock. In the mid-20th century, investors held a typical company's stock for a few years. In 2011, the average US stock was held for 22 seconds.

Over the past decade, algorithmic trading, which is done by machine traders, has overtaken the financial markets. It is now accountable for most of the trading activity on Wall Street, and it generates more than 70 percent of total trade volume in the US. Today, all the large banks, pension funds and mutual funds use algorithms to execute their trading orders.

Some algorithms do proprietary trading. They sell and buy individual stocks. Other algorithms execute large trades. They break large orders into smaller orders and arrange them in the way that the orders become hidden from the rest of the market.

Some algorithms are designed for predatory trading. They search for large orders in order to front-run them.

High-frequency trading (HFT) is one of the types of algorithmic trading. Computer algorithms used by HFT firms are also called "*algos*" or "*high-frequency traders (HFTs)*," and scientists, who design algos, are informally called "quants." Many algos are designed by HFT firms for predatory trading. HFT firms also use super-fast computers and super-fast connections. Thanks to all these technological advantages, HFTs can execute trades in a fraction of a second, and they can front-run mutual funds, pension funds, and other large market players.

Although high-frequency trading firms rely on high-speed computers, they were not the pioneers of computerized trading. Computerized trading existed long before high-frequency trading, when two exchanges dominated Wall Street: the NYSE and NASDAQ.

By the end of 1980s and into the 1990s, developments in information technology (IT) have brought an electronic revolution to the market, enabling traders to remotely access multiple trading venues. At that time, NASDAQ used middlemen called *market makers* in order to smooth out the demand for buying and selling. Traditional market makers bought and sold stocks continuously during the trading day.

For example, at some moment of time there could be a seller of shares on the market, but no buyers. The market makers would buy the shares from the seller, hold them temporarily and then sell to the buyers when they came to the market. For the NYSE, so-called "specialist" firms matched buyers and sellers. For a long time, these firms have been suspected of front-running traders and making money by cheating other investors.

In 1986, Josh Levine began developing computer programs that would compete against NASDAQ market makers. His work led to the creation of an "off-exchange" exchange called the Island or more generally, an electronic communications network (ECN). It allowed traders to directly trade with each other, while avoiding the market makers. Other ECNs, such as Archipelago, were designed and launched soon after the creation of Island.

In the early 2000s, more and more firms were trading stocks as well as other securities, electronically, frequently by using ECNs. The NYSE and NASDAQ found themselves lagging behind in electronic trading. But in 2005, NASDAQ purchased Inet, which was the result of the merger of Island with another ECN, Instinet. At the same time, the NYSE purchased Archipelago, which had become known as Arca. Nowadays, NASDAQ's matching engine is really an advanced version of the one created by Josh Levine.

In the 2000s, computerized trading also benefited from "decimalization," when the trading of stocks in fractions-of-a-dollar increments was changed to penny-wide increments. The trading environment changed considerably after the new regulation was adopted in 2007. The regulation was designed to increase transparency. It required brokers to offer their clients the best possible price through all U.S. exchanges. To achieve this, price information would have to be synchronized.

Since that time, high-frequency trading firms have spent tremendous resources developing infrastructure, as well as the computer algorithms, in order to achieve extremely small advantages in time. Billions of dollars have been spent on construction of gigantic automated data centers. Mountains have been drilled in order to run straight fiber-optic cables.

Large-scale investments have also been made in microwave transmission systems in order to switch from fiber-optic cables to microwave technology for long-distance networking. The transition to microwave transmission technology has become particularly important because data travels almost 30 percent slower through fiber-optic cable than through microwave transmission in the atmosphere.

All this technology gave HFT firms an overwhelming advantage over non-HFT traders. Within two years of the Flash Crash of 2010, HFT firms' activity accounted for nearly 70 percent of market activity in the U.S. and 40 percent of market activity in Europe.

Today, we have financial markets divided into different levels. At one level, human traders and machine traders continue to co-exist and trade with one another. At another level, where humans cannot keep up with machine traders, all the trades are executed by algos.

As algorithmic trading keeps advancing, human traders are losing control over the market.

2. HFT and Its Algos Are Rising

Both HFT firms and traditional institutional investors, such as mutual finds and pension funds, use algorithms to do trading. But traditional institutional investors usually use them to purchase a stock for long-term investment. HFT firms do not care about long-term investment. Algos used by HFT firms can execute a large number of trades, usually within microseconds. HFT firms hold a stock for a very short period, sometimes just for a few seconds.

The recent sharp increase in trading volume in the US stock market has been driven by HFT firms. Today, only a few hundred firms out of approximately 20,000 trading in the US markets are HFT firms, and they are accountable for more than 70 percent of the trading volume in the US stock market, making tens of billions of dollars profits every year.

In the 1990s, the computerization of trading allowed individual investors to benefit from equally speedy access to markets, and it also lowered transaction costs. Today, non-HFT investors have lost these benefits because of special arrangements, including co-location services and special trade data feeds that give HFT firms great advantage over non-HFT traders. (Co-location refers to placing a firm's computers as close to the exchanges' servers as possible.)

Michael Lewis investigated the negative impact of HFT in his famous book Flash Boys: A Wall Street Revolt. In his book, Lewis writes that high-frequency trading is similar to cheating at poker. He identified the HFTs' trading advantage that depends on two different strategies.

One strategy is applied when HFTs keep placing buy or sell orders for small amounts at several exchanges, and they "watch" how their orders are filled in order to detect any large investor who might try to execute a larger order.

Once they detect a large investor, they front-run that investor. Another HFT strategy involves front-running unsuspecting non-HFT investors in dark pools, which are typically established by banks.

In his book, Lewis points out that HFTs distort the market by using their front-running technique. They obtain information about non-HFT investors' orders, buy a stock before the non-HFT investor does and then re-sell it to the investor at a higher price. According to Lewis, HFT firms steal from 5 to 15 billion dollars from investors every year.

Lewis thinks that the regulators are unable to resolve HFT-related issues. And he is right.

In May 2011, Mary Shapiro, the Chairwoman of the SEC from January 2009 through December 2012, admitted that "the Commission's tools for collecting data and surveilling our markets are wholly inadequate to the task of overseeing the largest equity markets in the world." If the SEC cannot monitor the algos, then it cannot regulate them.

Lewis suggests that the market can act as a self-correcting system fixing its own problems. In other words, he proposes to control fast-developing technology using another technology, moving further from the "manned" market to the "unmanned" market.

In his book, Lewis only briefly talks about the Flash Crash. Yet, the Flash Crash points to a serious problem associated with HFT and algorithmic trading in general. The name of this problem is instability in financial markets.

3. The Flash Crash and Other Surprises

Whereas HFT firms may be steadily stealing money from non-HFT investors, market instability created by algos can reduce or even destroy investments of retail investors and institutional investors, such as mutual funds and pension funds. In 2010, the Flash Crash demonstrated how quickly this could happen.

"Flash Crash" is a name commonly used for the trading event that happened on May 6, 2010. On that day, the US stock market experienced one of the most severe price drops in its history. The Dow Jones Industrial Average Index (DJIA) dropped by 900 points in less than 5 minutes, and then it recovered most of its losses in the next 15 minutes.

During the Flash Crash, chaos ruled the market. Shares of Apple, for example, were sold for 100,000 USD per share, and shares of Accenture were offered at a penny per share.

Although the Flash Crash lasted less than 30 minutes, it erased more than a trillion dollars in market capitalization and triggered cancellation of more than 20,000 trades. And it certainly raised many concerns about the stability of the market.

Soon after the Flash Crash, Nanex LLC, a data analytics company, studied the US stock markets and found that the Flash Crash was not a unique event. Miniature flash crashes, which are abrupt and cause severe price fluctuation, occur in an extremely short period, repeatedly shaking the market.

For example, on April 16, 2010, the stock of Goldman Sachs Group experienced a 1.9 percent price change within 50 milliseconds. On February 2, 2011, an errant algorithm in oil futures sent more than 2,000 orders within 1 second and changed the oil price by 1 dollar. Its impact would have been greater if it had not been shut down in time. On June 8, 2011, natural gas futures dropped by 8.1 percent and then rebounded seconds later.

The increase in crashes that happen within a fraction of a second or a second coincided with the rise of HFTs, which are capable of analyzing trading information and executing trades in milliseconds, microseconds, and even nanoseconds (one millisecond equals one-thousandths of a second, one microsecond equals one-millionths of a second, and one nanosecond equals one-billionth of a second.)

Nanex LLC's research showed that the Flash Crash was caused by quote stuffing, which is one of the techniques used by HFTs to get ahead of other trading algos, and by delays in NYSE Consolidated Quotation System. (NYSE Consolidated Quotation System is the electronic service that provides quotation information for stock traded on a few exchanges.)

The SEC report on Flash Crash was based on the results of a study by Kirilenko and his colleagues, who concluded that HFTs did not trigger the Flash Crash, but their behavior during the crash intensified market instability and made the crash worse.

Another problem with algos is that they sometimes have bugs, which are errors in their software code. Practically all HFTs had experienced one or even more than one misbehaving and errant algo.

For example, in 2012, a malfunctioning computer program owned by Knight Capital, a financial firm, made the firm loose $457.6 million in less than one hour. Instead of being deactivated, the program kept on placing trade orders for approximately 45 minutes, and the firm lost about 10 million dollars per minute.

It is possible to detect some of the flawed algos when they get out of control and cause a fast and significant spike in price. However, some algos with bugs can remain out of sight, slowly affecting prices. It is possible that some errant algo can stay quiet and dormant for a few years, and then cause chaos in the markets.

Algos make the market intrinsically much more unstable and prone to sudden crashes. Moreover, the globally connected trading computer systems can spread a single crash to the markets around the world.

Sudden market crashes, as well as sudden bubbles, occur at a speed which is much greater than the speed of human reactions, and humans cannot keep up with them. Consequently, the SEC or any other human organization is incapable of monitoring or regulating algorithmic trading.

4. Algos Go to War

When algos interact with each other, their behaviors become erratic. When thousands of algos rule financial markets, as happens at present, the markets become unstable, unpredictable, and impossible to understand or control.

Since their emergence on the market, algos have been continuously evolving. At first, they were merely trade execution algorithms with very basic objectives and subroutines. Gradually they evolved into more complex strategy implementation algos that can tell other trade execution algos to execute a trade. The next generation of algos was designed with elements of intelligent reasoning, with the ability to learn from whatever is going on with the market and adapt the trading strategy to the changing the market.

For more than a decade now, scientists have been trying to develop computer programs that would create and improve adaptive trading algorithms. If such computer programs become a success, then machines, not humans, will be designing new algos capable of processing huge amount of data and making trading decisions in a fraction of a second. A market flooded with such algos would be very difficult or, maybe even impossible to understand, predict or control.

Along the way, the existing algos have already "learned" how to "wage war" with algorithms used by large institutional traders. Some of their fights are reminiscent of submarine warfare. Here is how it happens. Institutional investors, such as banks or pension funds, sometimes do trading in dark pools, which are trading venues that allow anonymous trading. The broker allows only a small part of the large order to be displayed, and a large portion of the order remains hidden. This kind of order is also called an *iceberg order*.

HFTs use special pattern-recognition software in order to detect iceberg orders in dark pools. For this purpose, they send small orders to "see" how these orders interact with large orders. In turn, the institutional investors, who are the owners of the large orders, use special anti-pattern-recognition software in order to make their orders undetectable.

In their pursuit of profit, algos that belong to one HFT firm have to fight with HFTs that belong to competing HFT firms, and their fight becomes more Darwinian. HFT firms create algos that try to trick other HFT firms' algos into making bad trades or not trading at all. One of the tricks of the war is called *quote stuffing*.

Quote stuffing occurs when algos place a huge number of buy or sell orders and then almost instantly cancel them. When they flood the market with such fake orders, the competing algos lose time processing them. Quote stuffing used by algos to get ahead of their competition causes confusion and chaos in the market.

Only HFT firms know how their algos work. Moreover, some algos are designed with the ability to evolve over time, so that even an HFT firm that creates the "evolving" algo might not know with certainty what to expect from it in the future. Criminals and terrorists could also try to design aggressive algos that would clash with other algos, which is why no one really knows how much risk the "war of algorithms" poses to the market.

Neil Johnson, a professor of physics who is famous for his work in complex systems and econophysics, has been studying financial markets for many years. Johnson and his colleagues discovered and studied 18,520 abrupt spikes in prices that happened between 2006 and 2011. They called these events "black swan extreme events." During these events, the change in the stock price was greater than 0.8 percent, and each event happened in less than 1.5 seconds.

Humans have limitations on how fast they can react to a particular situation. For example, it takes a chess grandmaster about 0.65 seconds to realize that that there is a dangerous development in the game of chess (for example, check). For a typical human, the reaction time is at least 1 second. The mini-crashes happen at timescales that are beyond typical human reaction times, and humans are unable to respond to or intervene in such events.

Johnson argues that "it is in such moments that a complex system offers glimpses into the true nature of the underlying fundamental forces that drive it." Indeed, his study revealed, for example, that during the period preceding the 2008–2009 financial crisis, a concentration of mini-flash crashes took place in banking stocks.

The discovery suggests that there is a link between what happens at a sub-second level and what happens in the course of months. Johnson suggests an analogy to engineering systems where micro-fractures can accompany, and even "pave the way" for large-scale changes in a device. For example, tiny cracks in a piece of plane fuselage appear before it breaks apart.

Scientists have begun to question if it is even possible to understand the market anymore. Johnson argues that the modern market looks similar to an ecological system with its own predators of various sizes. In this ecological system, mixed human–machine interactions are replaced by all-machine interactions, and computer algorithms play the role of predators. Johnson says, "Here's a real working system that we can study. The bigger issue is that we don't know how it's working or what it could give rise to."

Meanwhile, this ecosystem expands all around the planet as financial markets become global and interconnected. Market instability caused by a war of algorithms in one part of the world can negatively affect financial markets worldwide.

5. Goodbye HFT, Hello HIT!

In is not just about high speed and front-running anymore. High-frequency trading is being gradually replaced by high-intelligence trading (HIT) that relies on computers, servers and algos capable of searching and analyzing useful data, making decisions and doing the trading. HIT technology is not limited to increasing speed and reducing latency. It becomes an intelligent electronic trader that can analyze huge amounts of data and trade faster than humans ever could.

There is a practical reason why HFT and other electronic trading firms are making the transition to HIT: a set of "good old" HFTs is not sufficient to make big money anymore. Today, computers, or machine traders, do not have to be the fastest, but they have to be the smartest. They have to use data search, mathematical modelling and artificial intelligence techniques, including machine learning, in order to predict prices and estimate where they can get into the trading queue before executing a trade.

HIT needs huge amounts of data, and the data can be processed quickly only by powerful super-computers that gather data from various sources, reading reports, analyzing collected information and making trading decisions. Consider, for example, how the modern market reacts to statements from the Federal Open Markets Committee (FOMC) of the US Federal Reserve Bank.

Once the FOMC releases its statement, it takes about 150 milliseconds for the report to reach Chicago and for computers to generate and send trading instructions to the exchanges in New York, and then to other computers to execute the trades.

Information processed by machine traders is not limited to market data. HIT computers and servers also collect and analyze information from news feed data and even from social media. From Twitter feeds, HIT computers and servers can learn, for instance, about changes in the real estate markets. Within milliseconds, HIT technology can parse natural language and make trading decisions using obtained information.

For example, IBM's Power Systems servers work together with Linux, an open source operating system, in order to handle huge amounts of data for financial and to "digest" information from various sources, including government policy and economic news, as well as social media websites.

6. Elementary, My Dear Watson!

Today, scientists work on designing computer technology that will be able to understand trading information as well as non-numeric information, including written news, discussions on social media websites, phone conversations, radio programs, videos and podcasts. The key word here is "understand." It tells us about the rise of certain elements of artificial intelligence.

To get a better idea of how high-intelligence trading can be empowered by artificial intelligence, let us take a more in-depth look at Watson. In February 2011, Watson defeated two highly-experienced players in the game of *Jeopardy*. This victory drew a lot of media attention because Watson is not a human being, but a super-computer designed by IBM.

During the *Jeopardy* game, the questions were delivered to Watson in the form of text. In order to answer the questions, Watson was allowed to use 200 million pages of information from various sources stored in its memory. It had only seconds to analyze a question, search through those 200 million pages for possible answers, and then to decide which answer would be the right one.

Watson was made of ten racks of ten Power 750 servers, and during the game, its hardware was kept away from other human participants because its cooling system was continuously producing loud noise. In the years following the game, Watson got faster and lost weight. Today, Watson is almost 3 times faster than it was in 2011 and about 15 times smaller. It is about the size of a drawer in a refrigerator.

Whereas IBM officially calls Watson a cognitive computing system, Watson might be considered as a first-generation artificial intelligence entity that can read and understand natural language (a voice-recognition feature can enable it to listen as well). Watson can generate and evaluate hypotheses based on data provided and learn from its interactions with humans and from any other sources of information it can access.

Healthcare is the first industry that Watson is being tailored for. Today, medical knowledge of the electronic "Doctor" Watson is similar to that of a first-year medical student. IBM hopes that, in the future, Watson will be able to assist with making diagnosis and treatment decisions.

But IBM does not plan to limit Watson to medicine. Watson can bring great profits when used in business and finance, including trading. IBM is already working with financial institutions to teach Watson the business of banking. For example, together with Citigroup, IBM uses Watson for restructuring interactions between the bank and its customers and enabling financial experts "to make better business decisions."

A company named Modulus is developing the SharpeMind application based on Watson technology with the objective of making it a trading expert. The company announced that the SharpeMind could read and analyze 10 million financial reports in 15 seconds. Such a speed delivers great advantages, especially when the amount of financial information is increasing by about 70 percent each year. For example, Reuters releases 9,000pages of financial news daily.

The SharpeMind analyzes tremendous amounts of information, including news feeds, governmental reports, and social media data, and it then generates real-time buy and sell recommendations needed for successful trading. The company claims that the SharpeMind will help retail and institutional investors, providing them with insights on trading.

But it is more logical to expect that in a market that becomes more and more computerized and "unmanned," it is much more profitable for HIT firms to connect the SharpeMind directly with other trading technology, leaving humans out of the "loop."

Algorithmic trading, or machine trading, has already become very advanced and an essential part of modern markets. It is being used by HFT firms, major banks and large institutional investors.

We can envision that algorithmic trading will be elevated to a new and much higher level when it incorporates Watson's ability to read and understand any information from the human world, to learn and adapt, and to make the right decisions.

7. Artificial Intelligence Comes to Wall Street

Today, technologically advanced trading firms and financial institutions already use algorithms and machine traders with some elements of artificial intelligence. Their machine traders and algorithms can learn, evolve and create their own rules. As artificial intelligence begins to extend its reach into the financial markets even beyond trading algorithms, human presence in the market may become irrelevant.

Artificial intelligence begins with powerful computing systems that utilize machine learning. Unlike most software programs and algorithms that thoughtlessly follow their existing subroutines, machine learning means that machines, their software and algorithms continuously collect and analyze information, and they adjust their behavior in accordance with knowledge gained from their previous experience.

There are financial firms that already use machines with some elements of artificial intelligence as advisors. For example, in spring 2014, Deep Knowledge Ventures, a Hong Kong-based venture capital firm, appointed a computer program, an algorithm named Vital, to its Board of Directors and granted it full voting rights. The company announced that Vital has the capability to analyze financial trends and forecast successful investments.

Indeed, we are witnessing the emergence of the next generation of artificial intelligence algorithms. These algorithms can change trading strategy using information about market conditions and knowledge of the interactions between trading orders and the market. They have their limitations, however, because they do not see and do not understand the full picture of the dynamic behavior of the market. But this can change as some technological firms and research centers now look into developing artificial neural networks.

Artificial neural networks are designed to simulate the operation of the human brain. They are built from a large number of processors connected together in a manner similar to the connections between neurons.

Artificial neural networks can become more and more intelligent by learning from huge amounts of data and by learning from their own experience. They are taking an important step toward the emergence of artificial intelligence that comprises technology duplicating the functions of the human brain.

8. Google's Quest for Artificial Intelligence

Our discussion of possible issues arising with the emergence of artificial intelligence would not be complete without mentioning Google's quest for artificial intelligence.

Google is currently working on establishing the largest artificial intelligence research facility on the planet. Google has already acquired many machine-learning and robotics companies, including Boston Dynamics, the company that designs military robots, as well as Nest Labs, the British artificial intelligence company, DeepMind, and many others. Google also hired Geoff Hinton, a British computer scientist and one of the world's top experts on artificial neural networks. It also hired the former Head of the Defence Advanced Research Projects Agency (DARPA), which is the secretive US military research agency.

If Google develops true artificial intelligence, then that artificial intelligence will have access to a tremendous amount of information about the 1 billion users of the Google internet search engine and Google devices. It will be able to monitor and understand what users read, write and speak (more Skype and voice-over-internet, anyone?). It will be reading and understanding every email, every conversation, every document, every article, every comment that ever passes through Google's computers and servers.

In other words, Google's artificial intelligence will consciously know pretty much everything about Google users and the world they live in. Just imagine, for a moment, Google's super-fast artificial intelligence with a tremendous amount of information about everything and everybody. Now imagine that system connected to machine traders and doing trading.

9. Artificial Intelligence and Financial Meltdown

Ultimately, real artificial intelligence has to act like intelligence capable of learning and applying its knowledge and experience to a variety of unrelated problems and situations. Today, we are still a long way from creating anything similar to real artificial intelligence. But scientists are moving in that direction, and the time of real artificial intelligence might arrive sooner than we think.

Will it push us closer to the technological singularity, the event when artificial intelligence will exceed human intelligence? What will happen when that moment of the singularity arrives? Will artificial intelligence get out of human control and "take over mankind?"

After all, it looks like machines keep advancing, while the human brain has not changed its physical parameters. Paul Ehrlich, an American biologist and the Bing Professor of Population Studies at Stanford University, for example, points out that the human brain has not changed in size for the last 50,000 years.

Ray Kurzweil, Google's director of engineering, thinks that by 2029, machines could develop "consciousness" and the ability to do all the things that humans can do. He also predicts that computers will be a billion times more powerful than all the human brains on our planet by the year 2045.

Kurzweil's forecast about the technological singularity is something to think about, considering that he invented a number of devices that advanced modern technology, and he also made some other valid predictions.

In 1990, Kurzweil predicted that a computer would defeat a world chess champion by 1998, and his prediction came true when, in 1997, Deep Blue, designed by IBM, defeated Garry Kasparov. Kurzweil also predicted the super-fast development of the internet, as well as the creation of "cybernetic chauffeurs," which are now being designed by Google.

Kurzweil is an advocate of artificial intelligence. He envisions "the singularity" as the moment in the future when humans and machines will "converge" in a peaceful way. But we think that it is important to be cautious about Kurzweil's perception of "the singularity" as a great thing for all humans.

Certainly, it is possible that artificial intelligence will be able to do anything that humans can do, and even better than humans. But one of the things that humans have been doing successfully for millennia is harming and killing other humans. Human civilization abandoned the idea of peaceful coexistence and collaboration long time ago, endlessly fighting for resources instead. Moreover, throughout the world humans have accepted that the best economic system is the one built on exploiting other humans. And, yet, we want to create artificial intelligence in our image, and we expect that it will play fair and be nice to us?

What can stop artificial intelligence from taking over and even destroying humankind? Destruction of humans by artificial intelligence can be prevented by designing artificial intelligence that obeys the First Law of Robotics.

Proposed half a century ago by Isaac Asimov, an American science and science fiction writer and professor of biochemistry at Boston University, the first law of robotics states "a robot may not injure a human being or, through inaction, allow a human being to come to harm."

However, Louie Helm, the Deputy Director of the Machine Intelligence Research Institute, points out that, although Asimov's First Law of Robotics is widely known, in reality, it is not being used to guide scientists who are supposed to take care of artificial intelligence safety issues. Certainly, artificial intelligence that scientists develop today for trading and other financial applications is not designed with this law in mind. It is programmed to read, listen, learn and adapt in order to win the trading game and gain profit by any means.

Even if humans could add some software code to the artificial intelligence design in order to make it obey the "no harm" law, what would prevent artificial intelligence with super-human "brainpower" from finding a way to access and change its programming in order to break that law?

And if this artificial intelligence ever attempts to create chaos in human civilization, it might do so by attacking the financial world instead of using robots with lasers and guns. Flash Crash can give us some idea of how fast technology can trigger financial meltdown; happening within a fraction of a second, it cannot be stopped by humans.

We should also remember that even though technology might be designed with the intention of assisting humans, this does not preclude its inhumane applications. For example, Edwin Black, investigative author, studied 20,000 documents from archives in seven countries that reveal IBM's involvement in the Holocaust, where IBM was using its technology to assist Nazis with identification, confiscation, ghettoization, deportation, and even extermination of humans. Black points out that the tattooed numbers on the arms of people who were held and killed in German Nazi concentration camps during Second World War were actually IBM code numbers. In his book *IBM and the Holocaust*, Black writes that IBM's president, Thomas J. Watson, was personally involved in the IBM's program, assisting Hitler's violent campaign of murder. History often repeats itself, especially when we choose to forget it, and no one can guarantee that new technology will not be used against humans. Why not, as long as it is profitable for someone?

10. Are We Forgetting Anything?

When it comes to financial meltdown, the destruction of the market by artificial intelligence remains a remote possibility. Today, there are many other real problems that can cause financial and economic crisis. Their detailed discussion is beyond the scope of this book, and we are going to mention them here only briefly.

A new study, that was partially funded by NASA, has investigated the possibility of collapse of our industrial civilization in coming decades. The main causes for collapse identified in the study are unsustainable consumption of natural resources and growing inequality in wealth distribution.

This independent study was based on a new "Human And Nature Dynamical" (HANDY) model. Safa Motesharrei, an applied mathematician from the US National Science Foundation (NSF), conducted the study together with a team of natural and social scientists.

The study demonstrated that a number of important factors, including population, water, agriculture, energy and climate, have caused the collapse of various civilizations that existed in the history of humankind, and they can cause the collapse of our modern civilization, especially when combined with additional factors such as financial schemes run by banks for their private gain, as well as endless wars.

Glossary of Selected Terms

Algorithm refers to a mathematical formula used in computer programs run by computers in order to execute trades. Algorithms used by HFT firms are also called "high-frequency traders (HFTs)".

Algos refer to algorithms. Since their emergence on the market, algos have been continuously evolving. At first, they were merely trade execution algorithms with very basic objectives and subroutines. Gradually they evolved into more complex strategy implementation algos that can tell other trade execution algos to execute a trade. The next generation of algos was designed with elements of intelligent reasoning, with the ability to learn from whatever is going on with the market and adapt the trading strategy to the changing the market.

Artificial intelligence refers to the reproduction of human intelligence processes by machines, particularly computer systems. Today, many scientists define artificial intelligence as the study and design of computational devices and systems that can act in an intelligent manner, being able to perceive their environment and take actions maximizing their chances of success. The birth of the field of study of artificial intelligence is usually traced back to the 1950s, when Herb Simon and Alan Newell demonstrated a system known as Logic Theorist at the Dartmouth Summer Research Project on Artificial Intelligence. Logic Theorist was able to discover proofs to theorems in symbolic logic.

"**AT**" stands for algorithmic trading.

"**CBT**" stands for computer-based trading.

Co-location refers to placing a firm's computers as close to the exchanges' servers as possible. Co-location allows HFT firms to access stock prices before other investors receive the information about the stock prices.

Dark pools refer to closed trading venues that allow large orders to be traded anonymously. Dark pools hide the trading orders from the public. They report to the market about a trade only after the trade is executed. Institutional investors, such as banks or pension funds, sometimes do trading in dark pools, where the broker allows only a small part of the large order to be displayed, and a large portion of the order remains hidden. This kind of order is also called an iceberg order.

ECN refers to an electronic communications network.

"**Flash Crash**" is a name commonly used for the trading event that happened on May 6, 2010. On that day, the US stock market experienced one of the most severe price drops in its history.

Flash trading refers to a trading practice adopted by some stock exchanges wherein buy and sell orders are displayed to subscribers for a fraction of a second before the information about that order is offered to the public.

High-frequency trading (HFT) refers to a trading practice wherein powerful computers with super-fast connections run algorithms (HFTs) that execute a huge number of orders at enormously high speeds.

High-intelligence trading (HIT) refers to refers to a computerized trading practice wherein powerful computers with super-fast connections run complex algorithms (HFTs) to analyze the market and execute a large number of orders at extremely high speeds, within fractions of a second. HIT technology is not limited to increasing speed and reducing latency. It becomes an intelligent electronic trader that can analyze huge amounts of data and trade faster than humans ever could. Information processed by machine traders is not limited to market data. HIT computers and servers also collect and analyze information from news feed data and even from social media. From Twitter feeds, HIT computers and servers can learn, for instance, about changes in the real estate markets. Within milliseconds, HIT technology can parse natural language and make trading decisions using obtained information.

Latency refers to the time that takes a signal to travel. Faster speed reduces latency

Liquidity measures how quickly a trader can buy or sell a security at about the same price level.

Market maker refers to a trader who provides liquidity to the market.

Pinging refers to the HFT tactic of placing small orders (about 100 shares) in order to detect large hidden orders.

Predatory trading refers to trading strategies applied by HFT firms in order to earn almost risk-free profits at the expense of non-HFT investors.

Quote refers to the current price of a security.

Quote stuffing occurs when algos place a huge number of buy or sell orders and then almost instantly cancel them. When they flood the market with such fake orders, the competing algos lose time processing them. Quote stuffing used by algos to get ahead of their competition causes confusion and chaos in the market.

Scalping refers to a strategy used by HFTs in order to make profits on very small price changes within fractions of a second or within seconds.

Spoofing refers to a tactic used by HFT firms that place large orders without any intent to execute them.

www.ingramcontent.com/pod-product-compliance
Lightning Source LLC
Chambersburg PA
CBHW071804170526
45167CB00003B/1163